THE WHITE CITY

Tom Marshall

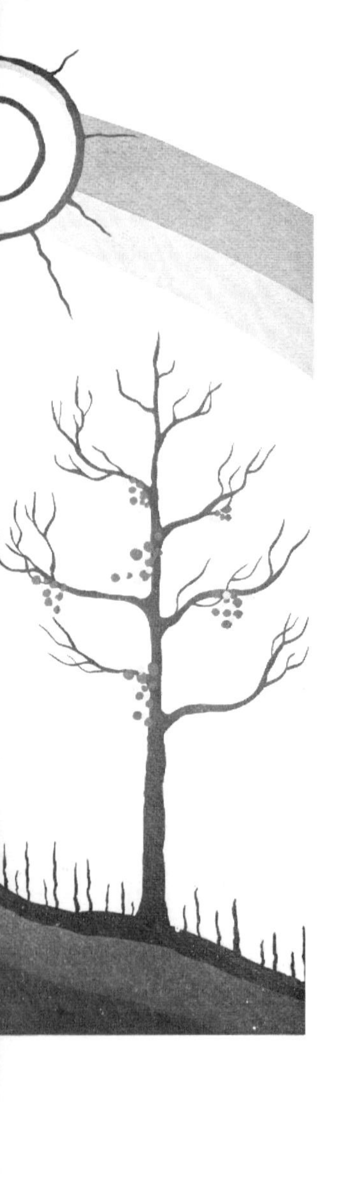

And now in imagination he has climbed
another planet. . . .
            —A. M. Klein, "Portrait of the Poet as Landscape"

How do you know but every Bird that cuts the airy way,
Is an Immense World of Delight, closed by your senses five?
            —William Blake, "The Marriage of Heaven and Hell"

. . . Ezra Pound and T. S. Eliot
fighting in the captain's tower
while calypso singers laugh at them
and fishermen hold flowers. . .
                    —Bob Dylan, "Desolation Row"

There is another world, but it is in this one.
                            —Paul Eluard

5

This is the *book of air* that completes the quartet of earth, air, fire and water. I associate air with lightness, openness, joy, the ranging mind, art, psychic space: transcendence. I knew that I would have to get out into the open spaces of the world and the psyche—they are not ultimately separable —in order to write this book. I didn't know just where this journey was going to take me, but it seems, in retrospect, inevitable that one of the several destinations—expressed here in the loose sequence "Out There: objects disposed, fragmenting, in our own space"—should be in Indian legend and myth, some traditional, some divined. (Glooskap, for instance, is a demi-god of the Micmacs on the east coast, but I've extended his territory to at least half of Canada.) I wonder now that I didn't get into this area ten years before in *The Silences of Fire*, since I was then (and subsequently) involved in some of the same symbols and insights.

One can be chosen by a place before one is conscious of its psychic history. Perhaps we newcomers of recent centuries have, in spite of our sins, begun at last to soak up some of the psychic energies of this space. Certainly Emily Carr did. Many, it seems to me, are now at home, frightened no longer (though the world remains, as always, rich and dangerous), content to be dust here.

—TOM MARSHALL

7

OJIBWAY VISITATION

The red man growing
out of earth is also
a tree with arms
and lithe legs, a hand puts down
sinister-looking roots and his
eyes are wild
(with terror?) stricken
perhaps by light from
a pale blue disc whose
rays are spears piercing
the weasel at his side—
hare and birds and tree
transparent, x-rayed
red world on blue sky:
sombre rainbow.

Looking at the Indian
silkscreen there
on the wall my own eyes
now begin to give off light
and power, I am haunted
by presence, an unseen guest
in another room or just
outside the window quiet in the
driveway though I cannot
see him, haunted or
hunted as I have been
these few times over
30 or more years, it is
happening again, I
am hunted again by my "self."

9

I

TREKKING OUT

DREAM OF WILFRID OWEN: 18 DECEMBER, 1973

For A.K.M. and G.S.F.

I have seen him in a dream
with bayonet

a blue uniform
striding steadily uphill

running at huge
stuffed Moloch sitting on hillside.

Moloch is made of sawdust.
Aquarius approaches.

Moloch looks like Buddha.
Motionless.

The blue soldier hacks
off one fat leg at the thigh.

11

VISITING TRENT UNIVERSITY

For Arthur Smith

Walking by locks.

Snow,
patches of brown, a German
Shepherd turning and bounding,
slime-green waterfalls falling
over locks edged with ice:

an Alex Colville day.

Behind us the City
of the End of Things, Trent's
angular bones, fantastic town
I once dreamed of:

flying and falling,
swooping and
losing altitude
till an old man went by me
on a bicycle,
a bicycle in mid-air
and said "Do they let you watch TV?"
and rode straight ahead
steadily in mid-air.

Astral projection perhaps
prophecy.
February-grey
March sky.
Brown moment, warm
before birth.
Expectancy.
Waterfall amber
colour of a dog's eye
and over and over.

                    (A month
later damp grey day
of A. Y. Jackson's death,
insubstantial, shadowless day:
in Grant Hall great lamps hang
and swing a little in cross-draft.
Open space between yellow panes,
leafless trees moving. . . .
                         It was
a ceremony about
something else. . . .)

                    Walking out
from city's
deposited bones.
Vanishing.

Into snow, water.
Brown grass.
Trekking out.

13

I had another dream,
I was flying, floating
along green streets to school.
A child, myself
sits
at the edge of field.
He is alone.
He sees me
hovering above him.

When I look the school has vanished.

14

SPRING SONGS FOR KINGSTON

SPRING SONG

lakefog, ice-fog
eats the sun,
trees, murky lane

tomorrow
come, dance in
excellent rain

EARLY-MORNING LYRIC

as I move
sleepily
out of bed
a shaft
of sunlight
on my knee, my
stomach, erect
penis
gladdens me

15

SYLLOGISM

gold leaf invades
my room

orange cat is god
in green garden

ants inside glut
themselves on steak-juice

16

DEFINITIONS OF PARADISE

For Ezra Pound

orange lichen on grey rock,

willow lifting treasure
like the gold roof at Innsbruck

on robin's-egg-blue air,

brickwork and ironwork, artifact

garden open to lake
tossings its little lilac waves,

exact measure, just reckoning,

hypnotic brown, sound,
water over streambed

under bridge, god voices in amber,

the child says "ghost-bones"
in hot garden, meaning

insect-shells, islands of desire, images

compact and held, cities
gold and greening

BLUE MOSQUE: ISTANBUL

These windows are the broken
colours of desire,
cool promises of paradise.

And pale as heaven
the blue curvature, a
geometrical abstract of roses.

I remember this,
floating carpets and
the reaches of cool air,

I remember this not
as dream but
a clear sky matter-of-factness.

Or perhaps as
dream's mystical precision when
unrealized as dream.

I could understand: paradise
was promised.

The serenity a work

of architecture carries.

18

What awakening then
these ludicrous

bobbing chanticleers.

What absurd
incongruity: a prayer.

19

MYKONOS: A MEMOIR OF GREEK EASTER

I

Bells and fireworks,
flowers.

    Windmills,

        girls
        washing beneath.

Terraced hills,
no vines.

        Easter-white
        houses

    floating on pure green   blazing blue

Hobbled donkeys
wandering above the sea.

Lovely jangling of
guitars and voices

moving streets in
afternoon windows.

Lemonadha,
       honey-cakes,
              ouzo.

Men arm in arm
by water.

       Red eggs
       bursting from bread.

2

lambs' throats
are slit
while others bleat
and wait
in the shed
by the main walk

on the floor
there is shit
and blood

22

3

processional candles
church to white church

tourists drink
and gape

4

Mykonos
where sky burns
water cools

lambs turn on spits

hills lead nowhere
everywhere back to sea

island of sanctity

love hatched
from egg of chaos

24

5

Bells and fireworks,
dream-

poppies

flame out of darkness

my sleep
a dark red field

flows

rippling

vibrant   as blood flows

to Skyfather

25

RETURN TO STRATFORD: JUNE 1968

For Colin Norman

So green is Shakespeare's
country
one can understand
how he came there
his life over
and no illusions
left.

Perdita, his daughter
found
at Arden, Arden.
The moving between two worlds
the tension in the blood
the mind
ended.

London was plots,
assassinations.
Assaults on his mind.
Caesar falls and Antony rants
there.
Lear weeps
there.

Here
is green gathering, mild
twilight on lawn
where Elizabeth danced,
country matters, fields
and faithless wenches
spread-eagled.

Coat-of-arms,
ale and status,
local boy made good
by masqueing,
Prospero's mind moving
every third thought
to grave.

Miranda dances,
Caliban is known,
acknowledged and grieved for,
Ariel gone. Here
green remains, birds
call from wood, midsummer
comes.

COUNTRY PLACES

I

Matt's place has a hill
across from a wood,
Margaret's a river.

Al has a muddy lake
with village and gleaming church spire,
Kim a vegetable-garden
that grows and grows.

(Peggy too has a farm
I have not seen.)

Country places,
mind slows and concentrates,
forces regather.

Matt has cattle,
woods and a high grass hill,
Margaret a river
that flows in two directions
or seems to.

Al has an ancient dock
behind willows thrashing in air.
(Peggy has ducks, or
so her note says.)

Even Gwendolyn
plants seeds determinedly
in a narrow strip of earth
beside concrete.

2

Perhaps these are all one place
located in mind.

Light
held still and full.

Yes.
And no. Something old and cold
is there.
Cold as a Cézanne.
River's
motionless motion.
Chemical
exchange of energy.

Greenleaves whiteleaves
eating sun.

River flows,
wind moves grass on hill,
cattle feed in far fields,
white clouds sail on air,
fisherman sits on lake
face a shadow,
woman bends over garden
vanishing.

3

(Visiting Matt.

Trekking out to
deceptive stillness.

Summer.
Clouds floating in deep sky.

Dust settles
a strange car
blurred figures move
to house.

By the barn
swallow dive-bombs cat.)

31

GETTING WEST

small purple blooms
patches of white sand

white-spotted
antelope grazing

three indian
children stand
watching train
float past

beside the track
two gophers
nibble green
and chase each other

around them endless
window-framed prairie

dawdling by

my indolent devouring eye

IMAGINARY MOUNTAINS

For Lawren Harris

toward Golden

>then entered grand
>sphinx-like hills
>
>white citadels of sunlight
>
>fortresses, red ridges
>
>radiant darknesses of stone

Invermere

>evening light and shadow green rippling
>animal folds
>
>a range of
>squatting bull-frogs
>
>humpbacks making love
>
>yellow sky behind

at the Zieroths'

      morning's blue
      majestic oxen

      (light laid on fence-posts, grass
      blue-tinged cabbages

      cows and one horse grazing
      swallows gliding

      roosters crow
      intermittently

      sprinklers jerk)

lakes

      white peaks inverted in glazed cloud

getting high

      switch-back road, then switch-back trail
      to Swansea Lookout

      long lakes in long valleys, pines
      Rick the Ranger watches for fires

      tiny life, chipmunks, insects
      cabbage butterflies

      from below tiny house: white
      as a small Greek church

at Bow Falls

       riverbody
       charging

       far down
       foam
       surges

       sinewy

       sinuous

       flowering
       white vetch

flight east

       diminutive peaks
       Japanese under
       dream of mist
       less beautiful than
       striped flatlands

       later sun
       falls behind
       and twilight
       clouds are
       complex brain-tissue

HIGH-RISE EYE

sun city dirt
blowing on balcony

        scattered garden-plots
        vacant lot
        below fenced-in

skin converses with sun

        rooftops

worlds look at one another

        streets, trees, stadium

sky clouds
white blue moving

        downtown glass houses huge

downtown glass houses huge

          white blue moving
          sky clouds

streets, trees, stadium

          worlds look at one another

rooftops

          skin converses with sun

below fenced-in
vacant lot
scattered garden-plots

          blowing on balcony
          sun city dirt

high-rise eye

THE CHINESE EXHIBITION

*For the Chinese princess who hoped to preserve her body
in a jade suit*

I

jade suit greengold
in black postcard
apparently standing

Frankenstein's
monster-ego, floating
spaceman
cut-off

princess, really: jade husk
meant to be
heavenly camouflage

2

"Love fades like a
chameleon
into love. . . ."

                    ". . . lost laughter
trails like shadows
behind us and before. . . ."

Thus the young bard
romantic. Writ of cities, some
"fragmentary smile, some
broken bit
of half-remembered banter. . . ."

                        "Dying love
assumes new colours, to new shapes repairs,
emerges unexpected in new faces
that are unlike the old
yet like, charmed places
where ghosts and strangers
mate all unawares. . . ."

It was a sonnet
before I dismembered it.

39

3

Invisible: brain, bone,
cells, circuits, synapse.

Our bodies are
autumn cities;

love, memory, art:
smudged leafshapes on concrete.

40

4

From a room I see
the top of the Museum.

Orange leaves, rooftops.
Fall.

We need
cities, need boundaries. Princess
in her jade disguise

a city. We need
cities and we need
to leave them behind us, husks.

                    "Voices
of your voice
from cloudy street
or forms that move in windows
yet must meet
and focus in some smile. . . ."

We need
cities, are cities when
we move to open space.

EQUINOX BARBEQUE: 1974

countryside orange-bronze   green

oxygen to the leaf's brain cut-off

mist on Round Lake

fish snap at insects
circles moving outward on flat water
loon flying toward forest and
circling back

redsun falls

something makes waves on lake

mist thickens
two shorelines   one above   one below

(Jupiter   three moons visible
by telescope)

fire rises amid shadowy
gesticulations and singing

moon turns open fields to mine-fields

42

48 HIGHVIEW CRESCENT

A curved street in mid-air sloped down around

not much changed
except for street-construction underway

a crescent-moon of a street

on both sides old brick houses
too close together

not much changed

(moon-pavement's nether end leads
to Casa Loma

just as I was told
when I was six
30 years ago)

The house itself is narrower
than I remember
a glimpse of backyard
three stories

I can't go in, of course
or stare too long
though I see no-one in blank
windows looking back

I don't know who lives here

That double-window on the second floor
the study

from which I saw the sun rise and marvelled

my grandfather's study

That was spring

Up the street a small boy
dark, probably Portugese

He carries a plastic
milk-container

dawdling
inspects at leisure
construction debris
abandoned this Saturday

When I was six we said "giddyup"
to the milk-horse
and he went off automatically

The boy
has vanished around the corner

It is November
cold, brilliant

Nothing has happened

Down the street
two women
one black one Portugese
exchange commiserations as they
enter houses

In summer
there would be
lots of them
One would feel
how things had changed

45

Walking down
Davenport
I see
30 years
is nothing

nothing has changed
and nothing
is magical

(in spite of which the street remains suspended
relentless, eternal stone
like a cold moon
curving

Walking down

46

OROZCO'S CUPOLA:
ASTRONAUT AND ASTRAL SELF

man of fire
hurtles into air
for sustenance of gods   angels
what you will

consuming himself

I had not seen him
when I wrote
"burning man fall outward
into ardent space"
ten years ago

now I want to be a man of air

cool dry air

be consumed
infinitely slowly   beautifully by god

rising without flame or movement

entered by sun   water

                leaning over earth

                floating as trees

clouds house island planet stones float

eaten away by air

II

OUT THERE

OUT THERE: OBJECTS DISPOSED,
FRAGMENTING, IN OUR OWN SPACE

"How can the spirit of the earth
like the white man?"

Trekking out, re-entering, we find
snow, grass, trees, animals. Asking

forgiveness of earth and Indian ghosts. . . .

Everything feeds on something,
leaves on sun,
animals on leaves, men on animals. . . . Mind

feeds on universe as universe feeds on mind.

We are being
eaten alive.

Trekking out
we are vanishing into space.

We are evaporating.

We are antennae of gods or angels,
we are endless

        as energy endlessly transforms
        and redeems itself.

We are ourselves,

we are trees, we are the planet

cold and lonely. We are dreams

of having gone too far.

We are astronauts falling

over and over outward.

Vanishing

pilgrims on

Milky Way.

Men women

walking on earth.

the train ambles among vineyards
between lake and escarpment
how many times

grey cloud, sun diffused on brown field
patches of snow again

escape escape

again from Niagara

but this time is different   I forgive
the cliffs the quarries
the endless waterfalls

I forgive the people

who imprisoned me there   I forgive

myself for cliffs waterfalls quarries
my dust haunts

later snow
on ice with dark
brown water splotches

(winter

the tree
like a hand sticking out of earth
my dust haunts

The giant hidden in the waterfall

speaks to Nanna Bijou

Nanna Bijou   sent by Sky-People

to be saviour   (who sees in dream)

served by thunderbird   blessed

with youth strength and beauty

long-limbed and laughing   beloved

of the giant and the people   (who sees in dream

a great ship without oars

with white wings

The giant hidden in the waterfall

speaks to Nanna Bijou

warning him instructing him in

terror and destruction

laughter corn rippling no more

no music   to the north

he leads his people

to the north   (he sees in dream)

away from the waterfall

grief turns him to stone

53

The giant hidden in the waterfall

speaks to us

if we will listen

listen   the ships are sinking

white sails into white land

listen   Nanna Bijou becomes

a stone hill that sleeps

waken him   grief

has turned him to stone

waken him   (he sees)   the time is come

54

my grandfather lies

under Agincourt

clumps and hillocks   uneven ground

Canadian mediaeval   and I

shivered that day   in sunlight

dangling on a long

stem-lifeline out of

this earth

in outer space   falling

over and over outward

55

MORE DEFINITIONS

For P. and G.

black earth

                a woman digs up
                hay spread on garden

November sun

                fat white horse
                snow melting

dogs racing wide field

                ducks in the pond
                fresh breeze

house standing

                a tubular sheep
                who pretends to butt

in sunlight

                hay stacked
                in barn

cows feeding

foam of Niagara breaks   on Glooskap's forehead

he smiles exulting   in spray thunder

thinks north thinks   arctic joy

his necklace a   thousand islands

windflower snowdrop   spring breeze

Snow-Owl grows   in his white eye

57

Belaney became Grey Owl

Leaving England behind

That was part of the story

there was more

I didn't tell about

didn't think significant then

at night in the park

an owl descended and struck

me with its wing

58

One equinox Glooskap and Coyote met
at Red River's edge

Glooskap said: my servant Snow-Owl
in whom I am well pleased

Coyote chuckled
Snow-Owl was invisible

Is it agreed between us that we give
to him dominion of the north

Coyote howled with laughter   Glooskap said
it is agreed then

59

While Shakespeare dreamed of Caliban Snow-Owl
Coyote and Glooskap gathered at Red River's edge
dreaming of Shakespeare

                              It was agreed in council

Glooskap sent Snow-Owl
to study Shakespeare and his magic

(Snow-Owl extends himself becomes
feathery sunburst

                                        ubiquitous white
                                        energy

England shrinks into his left eye   At Stratford

snow falls but Will is not there   In London
he lies in his chambers
alone dreaming tempestuous white, endings

60

Snow-Owl contracts   Enters Shakespeare

Shakespeare sees:

fire flood plague torture forest holocaust a
blizzard tapestry   He flinches

Will dreams:

endless archipelagoes of islands
shaman in a tent   drumbeats (the shaman is dreaming
    Snow-Owl)
a ship sinking to weird music   white-man
drowning under snow   Man stands on
mountain-top sees   farms   sheep
trees   rocks   Snow-Owl in a blaze of trans-
figuration   pearl-
eyes encompassing everything

Entering again the eye of the storm   Will dreams
Caliban's revenge Caliban's forgiveness   A man
a large man stands   looks across a small lake to
church spire   under willows A-frame   stands

dreaming Glooskap

61

Will sleeps

he has decided to break his staff

Snow-Owl is dissolving into air, into thin

Glooskap chuckled (not certain he had won)

62

The world born again   Thick flakes

of snow

descending   Universe concentrated in

gold room   Intricate

Bach   distant Sun an explosion

on stereo   Caught up

in holy fire

Caught up

turning

solstice to shouts of joy   Morning

63

Walking on plains, on sky

Glooskap dreams all these things I say

64

senses stretch across prairie
sand, antelope, purple blooms and hills
become mountains

air thins

wheat waves, a god in-grown
(this is not
Bangladesh, this is not
the Sahara
where sand shifts
hungry for god, this is a
tiny archipelago
of affluence)

light-years from now
a train conveys
the still-young Emily
eyes rampant with

raw-space, intense blue-air:
fiery silences of her
acknowledged and
immense home

A young coyote and I met face to face in a field once. He had not seen nor winded me. We nearly collided. We sat down a few feet apart to consider each other. He was pretty, this strong young prairie wolf.

—*Growing Pains: The Autobiography of Emily Carr*

66

Home from England
its long exhaustion
of chloroformed birds

Emily came by
pitching stage-coach
straight to Cariboo

finding a cat, a familiar

to be touched to be stunned

by Coyote

67

Bands of coyotes came to the creek below our windows and made night hideous by agonized howlings. No-one had warned me and the first night I thought some fearfulness had overtaken the world. Their cries expressed woe, cruelty, anger, utter despair! Torn from sleep I sat up in my bed shaking, my room reeking with horror! Old miners say the coyote is a ventriloquist, that from a far ridge he can throw his voice right beside you, while from close he can make himself sound very far. I certainly thought that night my room was stuffed with coyotes.

—Growing Pains

68

Exuberant, cantankerous Emily!
Childlike Emily!

(How well I think
I know you.)

The good people
would not let
you be.

You struggled mightily.

For fifteen years
you subsided.

Coyote
would not let you go.

Child, old woman in forest
consumed in green fire
founting.

At last
totem woman.

Klee Wyck, Laughing One.

"The forest hugs only silence."

69

silent fire   green apocalypse
still and full fire gathering
around the fierce

old woman of the forest at
her easel   her dis-ease   her
ecstasy:

leaf and bough interlocked in
carved nebulae   cloud-trees
leaf-

galaxies that surge out of
void space   leaving off
on air

70

Emily vanished
into forest

Perhaps she found
her way to
the lost island
where Indian
power is stored

Perhaps the island
is in us
all of us who are

at home here

71

The shaman left
his power
like a mist
on the island

white on green

the island that
grows in each
of us now

the same but
different an
archipelago called

72

Canada: our green
rain-forest

cliff and
prairie windfall

water's
foam:

white nada our
nothing that is
also everything

73

Coyote howls with laughter

My poems amuse him

The trickiness of him
though he is tricked too
He opened the four
forbidden boxes

smoke blowflies

meat-beetles wasps

Coyote howls with chagrin

down turbulent waters

74

the two old women
bringing hatred death
the forbidden boxes
bringing age smallpox

having been tricked

bringing smoke-wasps death

his laughter echoes in galactic space

Coyote howls with derision

75

come back come back

sunshine floods the windows

darkening the mind's room, spring occurs

inside and outside, cadence lives

in treachery, a sorcerer's

journeying returns

form and fall, rhythms are

extinguished and changeless, city

disintegrating and opening, water now

breaks over cliffside, spring occurs

inside and outside, now

We are at

                    home here

everything feeds
on something   our Greek

                    Indians remind us
                    of that other home
                    sky

listen: every "thing" inside
is outside too

the tree
like a hand sticking out of earth
my dust haunts

                    as year turns

                    from shadowy
                    vast
                    planet of snow
                    to move
                    our bodies swelling
                    to golden planet

                    of earth   light

trekking out, walking by locks

snow melting   wakened from stone

and always

the voice of the waterfall and

the mountain

grass and animals

in the forest the wings

of the owl the words

of the cold water falling

78

A MESSAGE FROM THE GARDEN OF THE GODS

The fortunate places of the earth

are not perhaps many
this distinguished spring

The accession of light

is almost pain

To accept one's own land is to accept

one's death here

"The twentieth century shall be
the century of Canada. . . ."

Old universes, the ultramontane,
the monarchist, Pax Britannica
running down, old universes that
fall endlessly away to
become husks. . . .

Laurier: our Quixote

A dreaming pre-Raphaelite
youth rescued from
poetry and habitual melancholy by

a forceful doctor,
a girl in love

No longer to languish and compose
romantically in consumption

The bonfires and the torchlight parades,
triumphal processions in

Québec,
Ottawa, arrogant log-town,
Victoria's grimy but imperial London

The journey west by rail, crowds applauding

Worlds colliding and receding, shed skins

in which some still live

In 1904 Laurier said
"the twentieth century shall be
the century of Canada. . . ."

There are two kinds

of Canadians, fanatics,

Orangemen and ultramontane Catholics,
Black Mountaineers,
bigots and dogmatists, chauvinists,
separatists and would-be Americans and possibly
certain Vancouver poets, those who think
us-against-them, margins, black and white,
east against west because
diversity and distances frighten them,

and the other kind:

the secular shaman—

alcoholic, orator, spiritualist
who held the threads—

who rode the waves of light

magicians worn down at last
by the almost impossible task,
acknowledged legislators

81

Mental worlds colliding and receding

Old universes, old mental sets

Canada: a pacific breeze,

islands and innocent
roses, Laurier's garden,

rainforests, lodges, poles
of possibility

Gustafson said: "Backward
up against the possible
East, the
broken mountains of magnificence. . ."

(more magnificent then   as time streams back
like fire   closing of waters
direction of anti-matter
gods and symbolic animals   swallowing all
again

(there is no entropy   no second law
everything moves
into farther space   further frequencies

Imagine Canada backwards

A magic, a Chaucerian, screaming eagle
a veritable thunderbird high and higher up
might see

locomotives inching back
into foothills, plains

rail construction crumbling, film running backwards

Like distant clouds
buffalo float grandly, scouts watching
from hills

drought and wheat vanishing together,
men and horses—

fire and air, earth and water honoured

whip and gunshot and rope at Red River
receding, light falling endlessly away to

83

lakes, islands, height of land, trees

recovering their dominion, men

British and American in fierce

combat in smoky woods that slope
to cliff and gorge and river
vanishing

waterfall alone with its own thunder

islands blessed a thousandfold with silence

steeples and bells receding on the wide water

84

The grand gentlemen and ladies of France
their gowns and plumes and cocked hats askew
fading before our eyes into river

echoes receding, light falling away from
cliffs of Québec uncontested as
time moves two ways

(a backward flow, a universe of anti-matter)

débris of imperial wars cleared

85

(Descending to Fredericton with
orange patches in forest and
some months ago, juxtaposed:

rising over Halifax
abruptly to dazzling air

thick forest miles and miles below,
clear rectangular planes

sanded with snow, powdered like
Turkish Delight,

> remember
> sedate Halifax in torrential rain
>
> the naked girl decades ago
> directing traffic still
>
> the looting the fucking
> on beds in store windows)

86

all recedes
in waves of light falling
endlessly away
in two directions of time to

islands again, green, at the edge
of ocean one feels

Scotland,
England,
Ireland's pain

I believe that it was felt
long before the haunted men came

"The twentieth century shall be
the century of Canada. . . ."

A century of war and postwar

A century of slave-camps in which
time flows backwards

87

Imperial wars as leprous
Europe pollutes Africa,

America and those other Indies,
gold and rubies, an Aztec curse

laid on our acquisitive
Protestant-Catholic souls. . . .

Napoleon in Russia acts out
a conceit for cold Canada,

Robespierre and St.-Just
speak to the F.L.Q.,

Calvin and Torquemada and
black fire articulate us. . . .

Cogwheels, flowering black smoke
in England, God's tinker-toys

or Newton's, England opening
like a sick rose

Bess plucked from her
syphilitic Harry, Cromwell stamped on

until he is king, as Napoleon
becomes emperor, Stalin imperial czar

of all the Russias and all
their acquisitions, Ivan-come-lately. . . .

Elizabeth's England opening
like a cankered rose, the

rape of Virginia as the
remote Bermudas ride,

imperial Spain, imperial France, Venice riding
gorgeous argosies, Europe opening

like a multifoliate rose that is
blasted both ways in time. . . .

Imperial wars: the Crusades and
before that the marching beat
of fierce Roman rectitude that nailed, nails
us to the plank of order, always
expanding dis-order, not
that kingdom of heaven within, that
lovely spontaneity which
never was except
always in each
moment falling endlessly away to
nowhere, that marvellous
running line, that wave—

dis-order: imposed by Alexander,
Caesar and Charlemagne,
Napoleon, Bismarck and Hitler,
Stalin and F.D.R. . . .

90

Look east to the source

Even "golden-stoned"
Greece was not different

Pericles declared:

"our adventurous spirit has forced
an entry into every sea
and into every land;
and everywhere we have left
behind us everlasting
memorials of good done
to our friends
or suffering inflicted
upon our enemies. . . ."

91

But Heraclitus looked
eastward to Persian fire, and back
to Chaldean star-spaces,
Egyptian tombs,
Babylonian gardens and cities
that rise and fall by
endlessly changing and reviving rivers,
Tigris and Euphrates, Nile. . . .

East to the source

Zoroaster, Buddha, the Ionians in
their miraculous sixth century

East to Asian gardens, to
flowering stone and jungle death-cries

always empire, opening blood-rose

as light falls endlessly away
to other worlds and other kinds of time

The gods themselves, it seems,
need cultivation

the balance of that wheel of stars

perceived in Chaldean skies

This is an Asian garden, too,

this Canada

even in its pain

We are ourselves the gods
a tip of consciousness

like that of grass, water, stone, bird

93

This is our latest garden

our city

one of the fortunate places

on a remote, minor planet of slave-camps and wars

Inheritor of ancient pains
and anger but also
of that other widening life, that sight
of an eye opening on fire
that sustains and regenerates

Kingston: stone and green

stone walls glimpsed amid greenery

Its busy summer insects, its people,

their stone houses, transparent faces,

their sadness, eyes blinded with green,

white sails, bodies in light

persisting toward what new direction

what new flowering that is not empire

Citizen,

give your naked self

up to the green grass, to the air,

to the water, to the sun's fire,

to the snow and its blinding bird of light,

the white city,

the garden of the gods is here

95

ISBN 0 88750 196 6 (hardcover)
ISBN 0 88750 197 4 (softcover)

Cover: Carl Ray. Design: Michael Macklem

Printed in Canada

PUBLISHED IN CANADA BY OBERON PRESS